The Lively Garden Prayer Book

"William Cleary, once again, gives us a happy blend of holiness and imagination, fantasy and wisdom, humor and challenge. This book reveals God to us in the sacramentality of human experience."

— Anthony T. Padavono
Catholic theologian, author

"For a long time, we have known that we can speak to our green leafed friends in our gardens. Now in this book, the plants speak back! The reader will love to hear what they have to say. This is a rare combination of poetic prayer and a practical, down-to-earth gardening companion. A lovely book to be picked up again and again as the seasons come and go. Anyone who has turned the earth or even treasures greenery in their home or apartment will love this book."

— William Fitzgerald
author, *One Hundred Cranes*

"This is a thoroughly enchanting book. By entering into the imagination (and prayer life) of our garden plants and critters, Bill Cleary invites us to delight in our garden friends as much as they delight in us. Beneath its playful exterior, this book creates a sacred space in which we recognize every creature as a messenger of God, revealing the world as a place of wonder and love."

— Dennis and Sheila Linn
authors *Simple Ways to Pray for Healing*,
founders of *Re-Member Ministries*

"For Jesus, nature was filled with parables. Bill Cleary unearths still more of them in an ordinary backyard garden, and turns them into elegant prayer poems. This insightful and delightful book sheds light on many of our human dilemmas, and teaches us to pray."

— Kathleen Fisher and Thomas Hart
authors

The Lively Garden Prayer Book

Prayers of Backyard Creation from A to Z

William Cleary

Introduction by
Miriam Therese MacGillis

FOREST OF PEACE
Publishing

Suppliers for the Spiritual Pilgrim

The Lively Garden Prayer Book

copyright © 1997, by William Cleary

Library of Congress Cataloging-in-Publication Data

Cleary, William.
    The lively garden prayer book : prayers of backyard creation from A to Z / William Cleary; introduction by Miriam Therese MacGillis.
       p.   cm.
     ISBN 0-939516-35-7
     1. Gardners — Poetry.   I. Title.
    PS3553.L3917L58   1997
    811' .54 — dc21

                                   97-13947
                                      CIP

published by

Forest of Peace Publishing, Inc.
PO Box 269
Leavenworth, KS 66048-0269   USA
1-800-659-3227

printed by

Hall Directory, Inc.
Topeka, KS 66608-0348

cover art by

Edward Hays

1st printing: April 1997

Dedication

No one could be more appropriately my honored
dedicandus than
Boatswain

Edward Hays

on whose wavelength
I have spent many, many an undulating hour
a-wondering that he numbers me
among his friends
and shipmates

Acknowledgments

Special thanks to Tom Skorupa of Forest of
Peace Publishing for his reverent and
apperceptive reading of the original text,
and his beacon-bright suggestions. My
main sources for gardening information have
been *Hints for the Vegetable Gardener* (Garden
Way, 1981), *1001 Hints & Tips For Your Garden*
(Reader's Digest, 1995), *Devotions For Gardeners* by Jean Shaw
(Zondervan, 1994) and *Garden Smarts* by Shirley Goldbloom (Globe
Peqout, 1995).

Table of Contents

Prayers of Garden Creatures and a Backyard Theology

Introduction
by Miriam Therese MacGillis

It is a splendid joy to introduce a book that comes from a heart in touch with the teeming miracles of life in the garden, and a heart that also hears the voice of each precious food-bearing plant as it evolves from seed to the splendid sacrament of nourishment.

Surely we live in a time of contrast; unsettled times that bring forth both the darkest aspects of the human soul as well as its clear and creative grasp of the privilege of life.

On any given day we can find in the news or discover by moving through the supermarkets of our neighborhoods that the extraordinary miracle of food is under the most dire threats. From the corporate control of farming, with its ecological consequences, to the monopolization of the planet's endowment of seeds, or to the crass irradiation and poisoning of the food stock on which we all depend, there is no end to the destruction and diminishment of this most essential, beautiful and mysterious gift of the universe.

But hope is also stirring. We witness increasing numbers of people who are taking to their own backyard gardens or forming serious movements to regain control over the food essential for life. Seed saving organizations are evolving and community supported farms are sprouting in all regions of the country. It is as if we are waking from a long, drug-induced sleep and our eyes and ears are opening.

I hope that this little book will be an inspiration and joy to all who read it. May it also provide the insight, the sentiments and the inspiration to stir all of us to become defenders of the planet's foodstock. It is inexplicable that we should stand by silently as the immense endowment handed down through the planet's five billion years of evolution is endangered.

9

Whatever shall our children's children think of us who lived in this last half century while the care of gardens and farms have moved from the hands of people to the faceless, heartless realms of corporate control?

This little book comes as a prayer. May we hear in it the prayer of the earth itself, yearning to shake us up out of our sleep and entrance us with the wonder and beauty of her creativity. May these small humble prayers of the humus-bound creatures of the soil touch our hearts and spirits that we may be about their defense, protection and celebration.

Miriam Therese MacGillis is founder of Genesis Farm, an ecological learning center and community-supported vegetable farm. She lectures extensively on issues of ecology and spirituality.

Author's Preface:
Phatic Communion with Plants

Many people talk to their plants. Have you ever wondered why?

Or rather, an easier question: Why not?

A garden is obviously unlike the rest of the earth, a kind of Land of Make Believe — a kind of make-believe Eden — and when we enter such a place, we may do what we like, become whoever we wish to become. When we step into our garden, we walk off the map of the world and slide outside of this world's time. Growing things live by a different clock than we, following the cycles of the earth. Once the bulbs are hidden deep in the ground, the next tick of time is — spring.

In a garden we also become wizards with marvelous powers, we are magicians producing astonishing effects from elements that look insignificant. We create life, as it were, which then calls out to us.

We are totally in charge, we are almost divine. Why not speak to our growing "creatures" — who have become "friends"? It can be part of the fun. *Phatic* is an unusual, old-fashioned word that describes a brief verbal encounter without necessarily an exchange of ideas. Why not try phatic communion with your plants?

More than that, there are serious people these days who claim that the earth is in some ways itself a unified living being. Plato said the same thing thousands of years ago.

If these voices are even half correct, then there is certainly no harm in speaking to trees and to the amazing living plants around us. Many a gardener has learned to enjoy talking to the lively and personable inhabitants of the garden — or at least to enjoy humming or singing to them, thinking of them all affectionately, as children or companions who are in fact lovable in their quiet, generous, beautiful, lively way.

Some people play enlivening music, especially to their indoor plants. Who knows, our music and words and feelings about them may have a genuinely beneficial effect. Books on prayer claim to have proven these good effects, but, be that as it may, it often also has a wonderful effect on the gardener, gathering in the soul, quickening the heart, breaking open the imagination. Not that the communion need be aloud or programmed. Speaking soundlessly from the heart is adequate.

In *The Lively Garden Prayer Book* we imagine how the inhabitants of the garden (from A to Z) might themselves speak to God (*their* God), how they might give witness to their faith in keeping with their specific living traits, colors and purposes. Our hope is that observing this fanciful backyard spirituality — and the Backyard Theology that goes with it — will be lightsome and life-giving to lively gardeners of every kind, and warm them up to a more personalist and imaginative approach to that Land of Make Believe.

A Prayer Before Planting a Garden

A garden! There's a startling thought!
Dear God, dare I attempt the dream?
A dream like yours the day you sought
To make a perfect land and stream
    For Adam and his lively wife
    Where they'd be merry all their life?

I wonder: Would my garden fail
As Eden did, because of sin?
Or could I care for each detail
With lively verve and discipline?
    It would be fun if something grew,
    And thrilling if it honored you.

I'll have to pick a sunny spot
And clear the earth of every weed.
I must decide how big a plot,
How rich the soil, what kind of seed.
    I'd want squash, carrots, corn and dill,
    And flowers to give your eyes a thrill.

Then after watering each day,
I'd stand back and admire it much,
The colors, tastes and rich bouquet
Proceeding from my magic touch.
    But do I really have the heart
    To give it love before I start?

Sweet Gardener, God, was there a day
You first dreamed up the thought of me?
And pictured in some wondrous way
The lively garden I would be?
    I give you thanks for being kind,
    And hope I'm what you had in mind!

*The one who works the land **will have abundant food**, but the one who merely chases fantasies is a fool.* – Proverbs 12: 11

***You shall be like a well-watered garden**, and God shall guide you continually.* – Isaiah 58: 11

A Gardener's Springtime Prayer

Here are my hands, Spirit of Earth and Space,
Mysterious Wisdom within and behind everything
    that is
    and is promising,
Gardener ever ancient, ever new,
    who fashioned out of those colossal explosions at our beginning
    all the avenues to life, to its complexities,
    and to the communion we are destined for,
here are my hands.
Give them the skills of the midwife
    to put good order into expectations,
    to coax along the natural forces of life and growth
        that are already within the earth,
    and to help wisely with the harvesting.

Here are my hands,
    and here are my dreams
    and my faith in the promise of your worldwide project:
the web of life with all it might become.

Yes, I will prepare the earth.
Yes, I will study its mysteries and test its possibilities.
Then, yes, I will choose the seed,
    set it in a promising place and fertilize its environs,
    watering it above all, opening a way for the sun.

But only a midwife shall I be.

It is the seed that grows,
it is the earth and sun that urge on
    and feed its growing forces,
it is you, Divine Gardener, who give it its purpose
    and then ultimately draw it toward its fulfillment.

Take these hands then, and put them to use
so that in the process of gardening
I myself may blossom anew. Amen.

*This is what the kingdom of God is like: One scatters seed on the ground. Night and day, whether one sleeps or gets up, the seed sprouts and grows **though one does not know how**. – Mark 4: 26.*

Prayers of Garden Plants A to Z

Those who sow in tears will reap with songs of joy. Those who go out weeping, carrying seed to sow, will return with songs of joy, carrying their sheaves. – Ps. 126: 6.

Acorn

Hints for Lively Gardeners

A general rule for planting seeds is to plant about twice as many as you think you will need. Set the depth of planting by the size of the seed. The smallest seeds need no covering at all. Your novice seeds may appreciate a little verbal encouragement, aloud or silently. "Increase and multiply," you might say. "Show me what you can do. I'll be most appreciative and bring you manure more delicious than you ever dreamed possibł." Watch the response.

An Acorn's Agony

Nothing is more mysterious than our own potential

I wonder what is in me,
I'm curious of my core,
    A simple name: an "acorn,"
    But am I nothing more?
I long for great adventures,
Yearn for eternity!
    Dear God, who makes things great and small,
    What are your plans for me?

I see around this garden
Gigantic swaying trees,
    That wave at morning sunshine
    And stroke the evening breeze.
Two hundred feet they tower
And live three hundred years,
    Then, fashioned into building beams,
    Last far beyond their peers.

There's something to admire!
We acorns are too small!
    Just half a meal for a squirrel!
    We hardly count at all.

Sweet God of Light, please clarify
These mysteries we discuss.
    Why are there such intense desires
    In nuts as small as us?

Broccoli

Hints for Lively Gardeners

When green clusters of broccoli are in the tight bud stage, they are calling out for harvesting. Hear that cry. Cut off the plants, leaving about 6 inches of stem. If clusters begin to show yellow flowers, you have let them grow too long. Apologize politely, then cut and discard the plants; they will not be good to eat.

Broccoli's Blessing

Differences among us can spark immense energies

What a thrill, Creating God,
    To exist a bright green flower
In a multicultural garden
    Where diversity is power.

Yellow squash and purple beets,
    Carrots orange, tomatoes red,
Live together without conflict,
    Live in harmony instead.

Blending Spirit! Quilting Mind!
    Kneading Fingers! Weaving Hand!
Gardens are your holy places,
    Rainbows rising from the land.

We give thanks that we grow rich
    And rare! — for flowers are seldom green!
Happily adding one more pigment
    To earth's technicolor scene.

Carrot

Hints for Lively Gardeners

Carrot seeds do not mind being mixed with radish seeds. The advantage: Radishes come up first and mark the rows, and when picked, loosen the soil for carrots to grow more easily. Or if you prefer, use coffee grounds mixed with the carrot seed to help space the plants and ward off root maggot. Carrots should be pulled before they are even half grown. They are much tastier when small.

The Carrot's Gratitude

Commonplace things may be the most important

We give you thanks, Life-Giving Root Divine,
  Invisible Foundation, Ground of Being,
That in your image we have been created,
Vitamin-rich for growing, healing, seeing.

Native at first to European countries,
  Storm-driven seeds aloft and far were hurled,
Honored at home for health, we then became
Medical Missionaries to the world.

Easy to grow, sweet-tasting, brilliant orange,
  Slowest to spoil or stain (you be the judge),
Famous as food that hungry bunnies nibble,
Famous for making even donkeys budge.

We give you thanks, Life-Giving Root Divine,
  Honored to feel we carrots are so blest,
Winning someday the Nobel Prize for Healing?
Of all your noble works one of the best!

Dogwood

Hints for Lively Gardeners

In almost every climate or type of soil you can plant some friendly flowering tree that will grow and thrive — requiring no more maintenance than any other tree. Explore especially crab apple, golden rain, mimosa, redbud, sourwood, stewartia and, of course, dogwood. These will stand by you through thick and thin.

A Dogwood's Winter Dilemma

We may never know what is most beautiful about ourselves

Look, God, I'm freezing in the cold,
    Facing wind stern and austere,
        Leafless, fruitless, useless now,
            Save to wait until next year.

Once my fruit was rich and ripe,
    Once my leaves were red and gold.
        Now, my God, my wealth is spent,
            All my powers are growing old.

In my youth, just months ago,
    I would dance through every storm,
        Knowing I was filled with life
            And tomorrow would be warm.

Wine would bubble from my fruit!
    Leaves would flash on every bough!
        That is past: How should I pray?
            What is left to hope for now?

Beauty in my failing life?
    Ah, I pray such grace may grow:
        Red limbs still trace noble shapes
            Silhouetted in the snow.

Thank God, I am lovely still,
    Singing my surrender song,
        Hoping as the winds blow cold
            That springtime comes before too long.

Endive

Hints for Lively Gardeners

The outer leaves of the endive may be used without harvesting the plant. Your endives will not mind this at all. In fact, it tickles them. Note that an endive's mood — and flavor — improves with cool weather. Show your appreciation by telling them often how sweet they are.

The Mystic Dancing Endive

Some prayers are better danced than spoken

Rising slowly from the darkness,
    Curly emerald stems spring forth.
    When we hear your call, Creator,
Leaves sprout east, west, south and north.

Next, the corners of creation
    Chant a throbbing mystic song:
    "Grow, multiply and honor Life
By thriving now, both green and strong."

In response we endives flourish
    With green glory that enchants,
    Twisting from the earth's embracing,
Whirling dervishes of plants.

Laced with vitamins and iron,
Salads shape our destiny.
There we do our final dancing,
Mystics lost in ecstasy.

    Vital flavored, slightly pungent,
    With a taste that almost stings,
    Proving something slightly bitter
    Can enhance the zest of things.

From the wild of the East Indies
    We've danced all round the world,
    Happiest of dancing creatures
When your praise we've sung — and whirled.

Farkleberry

Hints for Lively Gardeners

If you want to encourage birds to enjoy your farkleberries or whatever berries you may grow, get a bird bath and clean it regularly. Birds use them for both bathing and drinking. Clean away all algae: a slippery birdbath will be unused. Spread a little sand in the bottom for better traction. It's a way of saying, "Welcome." A bird bath in a garden also attracts insect-eating birds, causing many of your plants to breathe a quiet sigh of relief.

Farkleberry's Dream

The most unprepossessing plants are often the most vital

Tough and sour, hard and dry:
Farkleberries still can smile
    To thee, Gardener on High,
    For you prize our rugged style.

We look lovely, round and ample,
Bright as gems at a bazaar,
    But we're saved from berrypickers
    By the ornery way we are.
Leathern leaves and prickly branches
Warn away the human race:
    Stony seeds may crack their dentures!
    Black juice may defile their face!

Make us into pie? Forget it!
If they get us past their nose,
    Take one bite and they regret it!
    So we're left to squirrels and crows.

Thus our seeds survive to flourish,
Multiplying everywhere
    In the southeast U.S. regions:
    Thus, rejoicing is our prayer.
Praise to you, All-Gardening Spirit,
Teach all things our lively worth,
    Till, to your eternal glory,
    Farkleberries fill the earth.

Garlic

Hints for Lively Gardeners

If you need to discourage aphids around your lettuce and other vulnerable crops, plant garlic nearby. Explain to the aphids what you are up to; they may cooperate, and your lettuce will certainly appreciate it. Garlic is ready for harvesting when the tops have died down, as with onions. Cure in open air and dim sunlight for two days. Then clip off leaves and store bulbs in open trays in an airy, outdoor place to cure until husks are paper dry. A quick way to peel garlic is to make a small cut across each clove end, then cut the clove lengthwise. The skin will fall off.

The Grandeur of Garlic

The most powerful energies are often the most hidden

Please excuse us, God of Grace and Power,
    If we Garlics sometimes feel divine.
How we came to pack such high dynamics
    Is a wonder of this world's design.

Humans long ago had learned our secrets,
    How we heal ill stomachs, joints and bones.
Slaves on pyramids in Egypt loved us,
    Marking our clear hieroglyph on stones.

Doctors in Old Rome and Ancient Athens
    Used our power in cures to ward off death.
Wrestlers at Olympus chewed pure garlic,
    Stunning their opponents with their breath.

Modern gardeners call us to defend them,
    Driving off vile pests of every kind.
But our most transcendent power is *flavor*,
    Making dinners taste and smell sublime.

Just a dash of garlic works the magic,
    Blessing meals with pure beatitude,
Rousing, strong, vivacious, holy flavor,
    Yes, a foretaste of all heaven's food.
To the choirs of God's most holy angels
    What a blessing plants like us can bring,
Adding to the music of their chorus
    Just a whiff of garlic when they sing.

Horseradish

Hints for Lively Gardeners

If your beetle neighbors are constantly in your garden and won't listen to reason, simply plant horseradish right in the corners of your garden and periodically along the borders. Chances are this will give beetles the message that they are not welcome. If you do so, it might be best to plant them in sunken pots since the plant tends to spread.

Horseradish Humility

Laughable names may mask noble beings

Don't laugh, beloved Spirit of the Earth,
To hear my name as I cry out to thee:
"Horseradish!" Yes, it has that crusty sound
Of "horselaugh" or "horsefly" — crude, rude names have we.

Rough, yes, but strong — too strong at times — and deep,
For my root word is *radix,* meaning *root,*
Hot, radical opinions fill my heart
In every garden-politics dispute.
    Down with those daddy longlegs plutocrats!
    Up with low income ladybugs and gnats!
    Should turnips mate with cabbage? Yes! I shout:
    That's how sweet rutabagas came about!

Save us, Great Spirit! Fill our hearts with fire,
Hot pungent-flavored peppy taste and scent,
Till at your banquets held on heaven's height,
Horseradish ranks as the favorite condiment!

Ivy

Hints for Lively Gardeners

Hundreds of plants have toxic parts: their fruits, flowers, foliage or roots. Poison ivy is the most common, recognized by its three leaves growing quite close together. Poison oak also has three leaves. Poison sumac is the most toxic of all. Don't try to pull up toxic plants. If you find a small patch, smother it under newspapers or black plastic. For large areas, eradicate with a systemic herbicide. They won't like it, but eventually they will accept the inevitable.

Prayer of the Poison Ivy Police

*Each creature on earth has its purpose
though we may never detect it*

Great Goddess, Queen of All That Lives,
We're your police executives,
Called "poison ivy," standing guard
In field and woods and garden yard —
    Wherever infant seedlings thrive,
    Needing protection to survive.

O yes, our cousins win esteem
On ivy halls of academe,
Reaching the tops of churchly spires
And towering homes of country squires,
    Costuming all the noble scene
    With glistening coats of evergreen.

But *we're* not fussy: Poor or rich,
If you trespass, you'll get the itch.
(Though few invaders even know
That first offenders are let go.
    We only punish the poor dunce
    Who's touched our wet leaves more than once.)

Dear Queen, someday our hearts may climb
Toward heaven's pinnacle sublime
And learn to reach up high and soar
Where hearts sing praise at heaven's door.
    But while we're useful down below
    We'll stay on guard through rain or snow.
    Beware, we *will* trespassers catch!
    Beware, unless you like to scratch.

Jasmine

Hints for Lively Gardeners

Jasmine — in cahoots with clematis, wisteria, climbing roses, ivy and, of course, grapes — is very frequently the chief conspirator in a plot to ensnare young lovers in an arbor — a favorite garden structure since the time of Rome. Jasmine loves to be reminded how sweet and enchanting is its bouquet, and will climb to almost any height to thrill an appeciative audience.

The Jasmine Conspiracy

Falling in love is a miracle, staying in love is another

Green Spirit God, who plays in groves
    Of thriving flowers and trees and plants,
        Come, watch a magic interlude,
            Come, see how Jasmine scent enchants.

Young lovers often linger here
    Supposedly to pick a rose,
        See, we weave snares to catch their hearts
        With mystic touches of the nose.

These climbing leaves create a bower,
    These yellow blooms lead them astray,
        Then, trapped in fragrance by surprise,
        Our spell soon takes their wits away.

See how their lips say foolish things!
    See how their eyes will stare and shine!
        Trapped in the magic world of love!
        Snared by the "Matrimony Vine"!

Green Spirit God, we Jasmines pray,
    Grant our young captives love that thrives,
        Teach them love's greater Magic Secret:
        How to relive this all their lives.

Kohlrabi

Hints for Lively Gardeners

Young kohlrabi love to star absolutely raw as a feature in your salad, or to be presented as a green side dish steamed without peeling. More mature kohlrabi should be peeled, sliced or diced and boiled in a small amount of salted water. Like most green vegetables, it is wonderfully healthful.

A Kohlrabi's Communion

Much that seems bizarre fits in perfectly — if we are wise

We give you thanks, Strange Mystery God,
   That we are weird like thee.
      Even our name, Kohlrabi, hints
We're nature's anomaly.

Like *you*, few know us by our name,
   And we are strange to see:
      Our leaves stick straight out from our heads
Like freaks in agony.

Our kin, turnips and cabbages,
   Fit any recipe,
      But "vegetably *incorrect*"
And "rabbit food" are we.

Detested, ridiculed and jeered,
   The garden's saints we be,
      For we live out our humble role
Communioning with Thee,
   Mysterious, unearthly, strange,
   Intriguing without relief,
   We are, like you, Most Holy One,
   Nearly beyond belief.

Lettuce

Hints for Lively Gardeners

Rabbits and other creatures love lettuce. Fence in your rows with chicken wire — or use a scent repellent to keep them away. Some gardeners interplant lettuce with marigolds, which have a strong scent. Explain the task to your marigolds, and they will work hard at their job.

The Hymn of Holy Lettuce

Too much religion can destroy a healthy spirituality

Light the candles! Bring the incense!
Bow your heads in pious array,
Kneel in reverence! Chant the anthem!
Saints are here, so "let us pray!"

Lettuce pray! The call is holy!
Lettuce pray to heaven's height,
Lettuce pray for saints and sinners,
Lettuce pray from morn to night.

Ask us lettuce, are we saintly?
We'll admit we're very deep,
Some whole days are spent in praying
For lost souls and sinning sheep.

Raised in four denominations:
CRISP-HEADS are most widely spread,
Then ROMAINE and LOOSELEAF LETTUCE,
And a fourth called BUTTERHEAD.

Lettuce pray! The call is sacred!
Lettuce pray devout and true,
Lettuce pray for bugs and beetles,
Lettuce pray till we turn blue.

Don't relax! You must pray always!
That's what pious plants are taught.
Lettuce pray from dawn till sunset,
Never praying all we ought!

When this lively garden's finished,
With True Life at last secure,
With prayers heard and safely answered,
Let us finally pray no more!

Marigold

Hints for Lively Gardeners

With blooms ranging from white to orange to burgundy, marigolds bring lovely bright color and ruffly shapes to the summer garden. They are one of the most carefree annuals, performing well from seed or transplant in a warm, sunny spot and in any well-drained soil. Tell them often how stunningly beautiful they are, and far more valuable than pure gold — because they are alive, a living story of drama and miracle.

Marigold's Thanksgiving

*We know little of the evolution story —
except that it is wonderful*

There were three kings of Araby
Who traveled far in hopes to see
    A Prince foretold.
Believing an astronomer,
One king brought frankincense, one myrrh,
    And one brought gold.

They found Messiah, God's own Son,
But soon his family had to run
    Rough lands to cross,
And as the mother held the child
And donkey galloped fast and wild,
    The gifts were lost.

But in each place the gold would fall
A flower bloomed robust and small,
    Sweet to behold,
And ever since that touch of fame,
We have been called the holy name
    Of "Mary's Gold."

So we give thanks: A kingly prize
Became a gold piece in disguise,
    A holy flower,
To show the God of earth and space
Is still a Gardener full of grace
    And awesome power.

Narcissus

Hints for Lively Gardeners

Narcissus, with their sweet and spicy scent and pure-white starlike flowers are very easy to "force." Set your bulbs in a shallow watertight container filled with pebbles, leaving only a 1/2 inch of their tops exposed. Make sure they are well anchored so that they can support the long stems to come. Add water to 1/8 inch beneath bulb base; never let water touch the bulb or it will decompose. Place the container in a dark place until sprouts show (8 to 10 days), then move it to a sunny spot. Bulbs should flower in 3 to 5 weeks. Be sure to encourage Narcissus, especially when they are young. Even as sprouts they can absorb a lot of praise and classical music.

The Adorable Narcissus

*The earth is so packed with drama
that only myth-makers get it right*

Come, Holy God, I have a moment free,
Surrounded though I be with devotees.
    Feel free to bow down to my yellow blooms
    And venerate my beauty on your knees.

My tall green self was once a splendid lad;
So beautiful I found friendship a bore.
    Mean magic made me this Narcissus flower —
    Which you, God, have permission to adore.

O Source of Beauty, Comeliness and Charm,
In me you show your Potency Sublime!
    Narcissus buffs are ever at my door!
    Their flatteries are such a waste of time!

Ah! But myself reflected in a pond
Is all it takes to make my warm heart soar,
    Six yellow petals round a sun-bright crown:
    Could any ardent lover ask for more?

Our noble line includes the Daffodils,
The Amaryllis and Jonquils as well.
    Too beautiful are we for this dull earth,
    We even have admirers in hell!

Yes, call us egocentric if you will,
To be *your* chosen love builds our morale,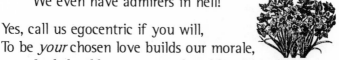
    And should you turn us humble with your grace,
    We could enjoy great fame for that as well.

Onion

Hints for Lively Gardeners

Weed your onions very carefully, since shallow onion roots can be easily damaged. Pull the weeds up and away from the bulbs by hand. Or use a sharp hoe to cut them off, but don't dig into the soil. Reassure your sprouts that you will not disturb them. A growing onion needs to maintain its concentration if it is to grow properly.

A Despondent Onion

*When we pray unwisely, God still listens and smiles
or cries*

Bless this old Bermuda onion, O God;
    Such a tortured thing am I,
        Wrapped up so in stress and sorrow,
        I make kitchen workers cry.

Though my outer skin's like paper,
    My next layer's thick and strong,
        Hiding all the inner secrets
        Of a life of shame and wrong.

Peel that layer off, Creator,
    You'll behold yet more disgrace,
        See the smallness of my essence!
        See the falseness of my face!

Shrinking now, still two more layers
    Can be stripped, the truth laid bare,
        In my heart is stinging harshness,
        Biting taste, burning despair.

What was that? You *like* my flavor?
    There's a wonder! There's a dream!
        Dry your eyes then, Holy Spirit,
        You've renewed my self-esteem.

Potato

Hints for Lively Gardeners

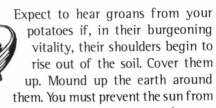

Expect to hear groans from your potatoes if, in their burgeoning vitality, their shoulders begin to rise out of the soil. Cover them up. Mound up the earth around them. You must prevent the sun from reaching the growing roots. Light turns potatoes green and causes solanine (sol-a-nine), a mildly toxic substance, to develop. Darkness is the natural habitat for all potatoes, even in your kitchen, a sign in nature of how growth is sometimes cultivated in darkness and solitude.

The Pouting Potato

Everything that serves humankind deserves reverence,
even the most lowly

From underground we cry to thee,
 Great God of Sky and Earth.
We are the most maligned of plants,
 Despite prodigious worth.

We're proud to be the Number One,
 World-widest grown of roots.
But, God, we're more than earthy blobs,
 We're also flowers and fruits.

That's what attracted Spanish eyes
 That found us in Peru,
Tall plants of white and yellow blooms
 With berries green and blue.

In joy we sailed to Europe then,
 But ended in defeat!
Folks feared we were a "nightshade" plant
 That poisons all who eat!

Soon we became poor people's food,
 Which much improved our worth.
So back to the New World we went
 And all around the earth.

But WE'RE MUCH MORE! We're Beauty's Crown,
 Not just misshapen duds!
The world should call us "Miracles"!
 Not just *fries, chips* and *spuds.*

Quince

Hints for Lively Gardeners

To cultivate flowering quince as a bush, just let all of the stems grow. But to encourage it to grow into a tree shape, allow only one stem to grow from ground level; this stem will become the future trunk. Cut away any lower stems that try to bud. Let it know each day how much you believe in it, how much you care about its well-being — without limiting its natural energies to become itself.

The Psalm of a Blooming Quince

Nothing exists outside the divine plan —
though some things live on the fringe

I have no complaints, Creator,
Just a small tree, weird and strange,
Fuzzy fruit that's sour tasting
Twisted limbs that never change.
    Still, I've joy that none can equal,
    Few can match my ecstasies:
    Juicy fruit, and bright red flowers,
    Cherished by the Japanese!
        Sticky seeds abound within me
        Wonderful for glue and paste,
        And my fruit, when cooked discreetly,
        Gives good marmalade its taste.

Known in myths of ancient peoples,
I'm a fruit — hard, sour and odd,
Proving even goofy creatures
Can find ways to honor God.

Radish

Hints for Lively Gardeners

Harvest your summer radishes when their shoulders first appear. Keep them well watered and they will reward you and not become overly hot. If interplanted with lettuce, radishes do extra well and become more tender. Radishes grow quickly, so young gardeners are quickly rewarded, and are something young gardeners can even eat right out of their garden. Radishes love the energies of the young and seldom disappoint them.

Radish Ecstasy

The circle of life and death is awesomely planned,
and awesome to live out

A simple radish, here I am,
Before your face, my God,
One leaf along a row of sprouts
Emerging from the sod.

As I grow up, in sunlight hours
I photosynthesize,
Emitting fresh, life-giving air,
Which breathing humans prize.

At night I dance and grow more plump
And mix the flavor groups
That make a radish just the thing
For salads, dips and soups.

The hungry often choose me first
To satisfy desire,
And I'm turned into human beings. . .
Till they in turn expire,
    And with their bodies sweeten earth
    That's helped them while alive,
    And give their substance back to the ground
    So radishes can thrive.

This one small creature sings your praise,
A child of love and chance,
Ecstatic to be circling
In earth's majestic dance.

Squash

Hints for Lively Gardeners

Squash are wonderful performers in the garden — and they like to know that you appreciate them. Leave winter squash on the vine until the stem actually shrivels. Pick them after the vines have dried but before the frost. Always leave about a 4 inch stem on each fruit. Never store squash without a stem: it makes them more vulnerable to low self-esteem and decomposition.

A Squashed Psalm

To be loved is wonderful —
even when it hurts a little

It's fun, dear God, to be a squash,
One's shape can vary widely.
You hang askew on mother vine,
Misshapen and cock-eyedly.
    Green, yellow, orange: a pumpkin form,
    Or flat, hook-shaped or crusty,
And summer, fall or winter squash
Grow equally robustly.

Squash once grew round as any ball,
But love made us too vital.
And huggers squeezed our insides out,
So "squash" became our title:
    They squooshed and squished and crunched and shmushed
    Till we could hardly harden.
That's why they call us simply "Squash":
The loved ones of the garden.

So bless my shape, and bless my crust,
And bless the love that squeezed me
Into the warty shapes I take:
It couldn't more have pleased me.

Tulip

 ## Hints for Lively Gardeners

Don't let the soil around tulips dry out. As a rule, water to a depth of 1 inch each week. Once tulips emerge in spring, sprinkle a little fertilizer on the soil around them and work it in lightly. They will be ever so grateful, and will try to please you ever after.

A Tulip's Plea

A lightsome heart is more enviable than any other gift

Look upon me, Mystery Spirit,
You in whom I live and move.
Yes, the gifts you give to tulips
Make this fickle world approve.
    Some say, "Gorgeous!" Some say, "Stunning!"
    Some: "The sight of you is bliss!"
    Yet you know so well my heart is
    Never satisfied by this.

Yes, there's joy in being gifted:
Tulips love to be themselves,
Yellow, red, white, cuplike blossoms,
Stunning on the kitchen shelves.
    Yes, 4000 kinds of tulips
    Flourish all around the earth!
    One can cost five thousand dollars!
    Much more than we should be worth.

Yet, I weep, dear God, for being
Only pleasing to the eye,
While less prim and formal creatures
Seem to have more fun than I.
    Dandelions go wild with dancing!
    Daisies swim in every brook!
    Buttercups chase every sunbeam,
    Never caring how they look.

So, dear God, I ask one favor:
Spark my heart with inner worth,
    For a lightsome heart's more precious
    Than all treasures on this earth.

Uva Grass

Hints for Lively Gardeners

Decorative grasses (like Uva) do not require a lot of attention early in the drama played out in your garden. Calm their fears if they seem bewildered, promising them a large role in the finale. At their peak in autumn, their stems become burnished copper, and they are topped with colorful seed heads. Emphasize this autumnal elegance by combining decorative grasses with such late-flowering plants as asters, goldenrod, blackberry lily and Japanese anemone. Seen in this context, grasses suddenly make beautiful sense and will hum in harmony with the music of all your more exotic plants.

The Uva Grass Bewildered

*Be slow to judge what you don't understand —
especially about yourself*

What *craziness* dreamed us up, Dreamer of Life:
What is Uva Grass doing on earth?
We're not like the trees, we're not carrots or corn;
We're just grass, so what are we worth?

Created for greenness, not function or taste,
Giant grass that grows gruesomely high,
With clusters of mammoth bright cream-colored flowers,
That feather-like, wave at the sky!

But so without purpose! Peculiar! Bizarre!
Plain weird, and preposterous plus!
What kind of a God are you, Dreamer of Life,
To invent plants as silly as us?

Too big for the garden, too gross for the house,
You baffle us, God, all our days.
Still we reverence the Wisdom we can't understand,
Welcoming your unsearchable ways.

Perhaps some observer with wisdom to spare
Could explain what we're doing on earth;
That in Eden the judgment of *beauty* came first!
Ah, if so, it unveils our true worth!

Verbena

Hints for Lively Gardeners

It's fun to train fragrant woody herbs into treelike displays: Base them in a pot topped with a wire frame, using thyme, rosemary, lavender, lemon verbena, bay or scented geraniums. It brings the bouquet up where it will greet you much more often and where you can respond. "Rosemary! How beautiful you are today!" you might say. "Verbena! Don't be too seductive or I'll spend all day out here." See if they don't reply in fragrant words.

The Hymn of a Verbena

However many praises we give to God,
our greatest is simply our own being

Five bright petals form a ring,
Four sweet nutlets nearby swing,
Hear Verbena as we sing:
"YOUR WORLD IS ASTONISHING,
    Great Mysterious God!"

Pink and white and lavender,
Sweet as frankincense and myrrh,
Chants each flowery chorister:
"YOUR WORLD IS SPECTACULAR,
    Great All-Loving God!"

What a joy to have been sent,
Healthful and benevolent,
Here to sing our testament:
"YOUR WORLD IS MAGNIFICENT,
    Great All-Knowing God!"

Though we flash red, white and blue,
Nothing we could sing or do
Would be quite sufficient to
Suitably give praise to you,
    Great Creating God!

Wallflower

Hints for Lively Gardeners

One gardening expert says, "The most essential piece of garden equipment is a hammock. Instead of getting stressed out that things are not perfect, go relax in your hammock and listen to the birds." Listen also to your beets, your carrots and your radishes. They aren't in a hurry. Tell them you trust them to do their best, while you rest.

A Wallflower's Silence

We are all poor judges of anyone else's behavior,
and often even of our own

I know not how to pray, my God!
Besides, I'm weirdly shy.
    Though I've no right to stand aloof,
    Born too reserved am I.

So full of fragrance, I should try
To dance more wild and free
    And live more turned out toward the world,
    Not so self-consciously.

Frankly, what makes me hug the wall
Is not how shamed I feel,
But how amazed I am
To be alive — and real.
    I'm speechless when I think about
    The wonder: TO EXIST!
    The MARVEL: that my soul knows how
    To live! And to persist!

I'm velvet orange with purple tint,
A proud part of the mustard clan.
Tall, strong, erect, perennial,
Rich food for beast or man;
    But even more remarkable,
    In fact, hard to believe:
    My cells give off fresh oxygen
    So human life can breathe!

All this is why I'm shy, dear God:
Life takes my breath away,
    So don't be shocked if wallflowers
    Keep silent when they pray.

Xigua (SHE-gwah)

 ## Hints for Lively Gardeners

A famous Amish gardening expert said, "When you feel downcast, get out there with your hoe and you'll feel better." In fact, you may tell your troubles to your onions, or your cabbage or carrots. They are alive too, and are, like yourself, just another part of Mother Earth, trying to stay alive. See if their quiet response doesn't raise your spirits.

The Mellow Xigua's Prayer

*Amazingly, the earth seems far more fertile and life-giving
than it needs to be*

Hear my prayer, Divine Creator,
    It's your xigua, green and tame,
Just a humble watermelon
Going by a Chinese name.
    Here I sit, a growing marvel,
    Full of seeds, red food, and sweet,
    Waiting for some human creature
    To enjoy my juicy meat.

But, dear God, I dread the danger
That my life will be a loss.
If no hungry human finds me
While I'm ripe! O, what a cross!

Still, *you* love me, Holy Mystery,
Fashioned me for noble use,
Whether small and even mammoth
With a hundred pounds of juice.

Don't let me go undiscovered!
Give me my one hour for cheers,
So my forebears will be honored.
(They go back 4000 years.)
    Deep in Africa we flourished
    In the days when earth was young.
    Let us serve till earth's completion
    With your praise on every tongue.

Yam

Hints for Lively Gardeners

One wise gardener said, "Just live with your garden and leave the irritations to nature. There's a reason for everything: there's a reason for slugs, there's a reason for aphids, there's a reason for us. We may not know the reason but we should be wise enough to know there is one."

The Shy Yam's Pride

*Everything on earth, however humble,
is like God in some way*

Hear this root deep down below You,
Praying from my hiding place,
Looking like a sweet potato
With an orange-yellow face.

I am shy, Great God of Wonders,
Blushing to be just a root,
Not a bush bright red with blossoms,
Not a tree with luscious fruit.

Still, you've blest us to be useful,
Twenty million tons are grown
Every year, enriched with iron,
Worldwide source of cortisone.

We're not proud, though we're born noble,
Known from the days of Abraham,
We call you, dear God, our *family*,
Since you're named "The Great I-Yam!"

Whoops! Forgive us, Wise Creator,
We presume your heart is light!
Even though you're Love Eternal,
From now on, we'll be polite.

Zucchini

Hints for Lively Gardeners

Zucchini are called *courgettes* in much of the world. In America the term is usually applied to various kinds of baby zucchini. Harvest your courgettes — would you believe it — at 2 to 3 inches, with the flowers still attached; slit them lengthwise and saute them lightly the day they are picked. They will tell your heart: "There is something wonderfully good about Mother Earth and all her plainest of children." Something very similar was said by the God of the Bible, speaking at the end of the famous Third Day. It's worth hearing often.

The Boast of a Proud Zucchini

Plants praise God just by being useful, fruitful and delicious

Here I am, Divine Creator,
One zucchini long and green,
Full of seeds for future planting,
Worthy of a king's cuisine.

Though my name sounds quite Italian
    To uncultivated ears,
Mexicans were first to prize us,
    Going back 9000 years.

So my history is noble,
And I grow superbly fast,
Giving energy to millions
Over countless ages past,
    Spreading wholesome human pleasure
    Almost since that race began,
    Just content to be called useful
    In the great eternal plan.

A Gardener's Autumn Prayer

LIFE-GIVING SPIRIT,
see my handsome little garden in its autumnal repast:
it rejoices my soul.

In the morning, I did sow in tears,
and I come home at day's end rejoicing.
It is all that I have been able to accomplish this season
with your encouragement and vital help every step of the way.

See where the sweet roots grew,
see the vines exhausted now from their abundant birthing,
see where the scent-laden blossoms once towered in the sunlight.

And the perennials lie quietly below,
richly endowed with lasting life and promise,
while russet leaves begin to blanket the whole bed
with the colors of high times now past.

LIFE-GIVING, LIFE-TAKING SPIRIT,
do you remember each of my failed plantings?
Had all my gardening dreams come true,
how decidedly more splendid would be this reminiscence!
Out of every seed or seedling that grew,
perhaps half came to nothing,
and you see perfectly each of my heart's regrets,
the disappointments, the heartbreaking bewilderment,
the loss of energies and dream strength.

Why? Why the failures?
I am not to know.
Is there to be a harvest of any kind, a reward for wild hopes?
A wiser and deeper faith perhaps, a darkness more serene?

Let it be, Sovereign Mystery,
Mother-Sister of sorrows, Father-Brother in dismay.
I look at my creation and call it good.

As for the failures, with the prophet I will sing —

Though the fig tree does not bud,
and there are no grapes on the vines,
though the olive tree wither
and the fields produce nothing to eat,
though the sheep are all gone from their pen
and no cattle left in their stalls,
yet I will rejoice in thee,
I will be joyful in my God, my Emmanuel, my Strength.
You make my feet like the feet of a deer.
You enable me to mount the heights.

A lively garden it has been, despite the failures.
Could anyone — this side of Eden — ask for more?

Prayers of Garden Creatures and a Backyard Theology

*They shall be **like a well-watered garden** and they shall languish no more.* – Jeremiah 31: 12

Seeds ~ Backyard Theology

Everything in the garden produces seeds in huge numbers. In this amazing phenomenon, the Earth is shouting: "Life and promise is bursting from me, exploding in energy for life, erupting into a profusion of power, pluck, vigor and possibility." It is the holy Word of Earth, and it should fill us earthlings with confidence. Though earth now lies injured, and is even under threat of extinction from our careless abuse of her, with vigorous effort, there is hope and we hear the echoes of this hope from every side, for vigorous life is bursting forth everywhere.

Hints for Lively Gardeners

On the market now (for the shameless gardener) are seed "tapes." While these tapes are more expensive than seed packets, there are some advantages to the tapes: Thinning is not necessary, and you can place the seeds exactly where you want them without transplanting tender plants later on. Also on the market are seed "carpets" — pressed soil embedded with seeds. The carpet can be cut into any shape to fit a container or left in the roll to plant as a unit. Seeds, however they come, are seeds — and are longing to produce new life.

A Housefly's Plucky Plea

I live in you, Creator of the Sky!
I am a tiny thing; you're God Most High.
Did you my shape design, my beauty give?
My legs, my wings, my appetite to live?

You did! You made me multiple and bold —
We are a hundred thousand kinds I'm told.
And plucky too, we all refuse to die:
Though swatted hard, we still get up and fly.

We're all alike in drawing life from you,
But different in the kind of work we do:
     My cousins Dragon-, Butter-, Gad-, and Tsetse-
     All have the mandatory count of feetsie,
Six — and dual wings to raise in prayer,
But after that, there's not much likeness there.
Some flies are pink, some brown or white or black,
Some are Chinese, East African, Slovak,
     Some pester Catholics, some get Methodists,
     Some go for Jews, Muslims or Zen Buddhists:
Yet we're one family since we come from you —
And move toward just one Destination too.

Prodigiously we're charged with pep and juice,
As geometrically we reproduce,
But in all ups and downs we give you praise,
And may you fly beside us all our days.

Earth ~ Backyard Theology

*An ancient prayer of the Native American Sioux nation displays
exquisite reverence for the earth. It speaks to God this way:
"Great Spirit Grandfather, everywhere I look, the faces of living
things are so alike as they gently come up out of the earth. . . .
Enlighten our way so we may understand this: to walk softly
on the earth — for we are relatives to all that is." To walk softly
so as not to crush any part of creation, even the lousiest.*

Hints for Lively Gardeners

Human hair provides a good and
cheap nitrogen source for your
compost heap. Six or seven pounds
of hair is said to contain a pound of
nitrogen — or as much as up to 200 pounds of manure. Call a
friendly barber shop or beauty salon. They may be delighted to fill
a container of yours from time to time. Remember to control odors
from compost by occasionally adding wood chips, sawdust and
dead leaves. You are simply enriching an especially precious quantity
of soil, showing exquisite reverence for the sacred earth we occupy.

A Lousy Day

Good God, don't shy away
When lice begin to pray.
One lousy prayer — should never scare
The God of All . . . away.

I've had a low self-image
For far too many a year.
Low self-esteem, all experts deem
A destructive atmosphere.

Yes, I need more upbeat thinking,
More self-appreciation.
For self-loathing, like poor clothing,
Conveys inner negation.

I find I'm not as far-out
As some might have supposed,
When I can't sleep, I just count sheep
Till my tired eyes are closed.
        (Of course the sheep I count
        are those I dwell upon;
        I dig a pillow from their skin
        and lay my head thereon.)

In human hair I flourish,
They call me "Parasite!"
When something's the worst — of anything cursed —
They say, "It's *lousy*!". . . Right?

Not you, O God! You love my essence,
So lice are here to stay!
My fondest prayer: with you to share
Many a lousy day!

Dung ~ Backyard Theology

*Why is animal life — including human life — so full of
contrasting elements: daffodils and dung, for instance? Is there
possibly some energy for us all in the very diversity we live
with? Dung is more than just a fact of life. It is a fact of our
spiritual path, a phenomenon full of revelation. Nothing is more
nourishing for a garden than dung, and the modest little life
forces within any tiniest plant has whatever it takes to
miraculously transform dung into beautiful, colorful, fragrant
and usually nourishing blossoms, flowers, fruits and seeds.
"Nothing is impossible with God." Or, as Faraday said, "Nothing
is too wonderful to exist."*

Hints for Lively Gardeners

Make Manure Tea by adding to
a pail of water 3 fistfuls of
packaged cow or sheep manure
(if fresh is not available) and about
1/4 cup of fish emulsion. Mix and apply regularly to all plants. This
will never burn them as other fertilizers may. Or, gather manure in
an old tea towel and suspend it in a garbage can filled with water
and fish emulsion mixture. Dip as needed. Your plants will very
much enjoy Tea Time.

A Dung Beetle's Love Call

Send me a lover, O Lover Divine,
The dung's turning gold in the summer sunshine.
It's time to be dating, or even be mating,
And ecstasy's waiting for beetles that mine.
    Not miners of silver or diamonds are we,
    But diggers of droppings from beaver or bee.
    That lovely manure that smells like the sewer,
    We find it far purer than spray from the sea.

My lover and I then would carve out a hunk,
Then pat it and shape it into a great chunk.
As if we were bowling, we'd start the ball rolling,
And into a hole we have dug, it goes plunk!
    What fun! What amusement! To tumble and creak
    Down the trail, living out our dung beetle mystique.
    Laying eggs in the dung balls where Nature will guide 'em
    And hide 'em inside 'em where no one will peek.

So send me a lover, Great Lover of Jokes,
We tumblebugs need all your graces and strokes.
With love, and strong dentures, we'll have great adventures
Without needless censures from finicky folks.

Rain ~ Backyard Theology

Religion is not really complicated. If it were, it would never be so popular as it is. Theologians can make it complicated — but only if they leave behind the essence of religion — which is our own spirituality, our own way of leading our lives. Jesus was especially suspicious of anyone who complicated a person's relationship with God. He simplified it: "Do not judge others. Follow God's lead, who makes the rain to fall on just and unjust." No questions with correct "answers." No difficult hoops to jump through at all. No catechism to learn.

Hints for Lively Gardeners

Cats and kittens find the scents of certain plants impossible to resist. Be good to them by devoting a sunny corner of a flower bed to growing your feline's favorites: mugwort, catmint or catnip, and kiwi. By planting these where you want kitty to play, you will protect other places that are off limits.

The Kitty's Catechism

Forgive me, God, I'm small and weak
And only born about a week.
    I've barely opened up my eyes:
    It's much too soon to catechize.

Do I believe? How can I doubt!
Mom taught me to be most devout:
    Cats once were gods for the Egyptians!
    (Now wouldn't that give you conniptions?)

Do I give thanks? Yes! Yes! I'm told
I'll live to be fourteen years old.
    Then die and go to kitty land
    Where, Mama says, the catnip's grand.

And do I pray? Well, I can purr
And huddle down inside my fur,
    Though mostly I just don't know how,
    And listen close for God's Meow.

Who made the world? I'm in a fog!
(I don't believe in God the Dog)
    Is it enough to hope and wish
    That you'll put something in my dish?

Ask my cousins — Jaguars, Panthers,
Cheetahs, Lions — for the anthers,
    Leopards, Tigers — they all know
    How catechism anthers go.

Forgive me, no more questions, please,
It's time for me to take my ease,
And lick my paws and chase my ball:
I'm just a kitten, after all.

Hope ~ Backyard Theology

Is everything on the earth really related? Are grasshoppers woven into the earthly fabric to play a useful role there? What about the plagues of grass-hopping locusts known to destroy a hundred miles of farm crops in a few days? The grasshopper on the following page assumes it has a role in the world, and no doubt it plays its part in the life systems it touches — but does that mean there is nothing chaotic in its way of life, and nothing it does that is genuinely detrimental to the overall momentum of life and creation? We have no perfect answers to mysteries such as these, but being a believer means ultimately choosing to trust the Divine Gardener. We choose to hope. Of course, grasshoppers have hopes of their own.

Hints for Lively Gardeners

Tell your grasshoppers clearly that, gifted as they are, they are unwelcome in your garden. Declare war if you must. Any wide-mouthed open container makes an effective trap for leaf-eating, warning-ignoring grasshoppers. Half-fill several of these with 10% molasses/ 90% water solution, and place them where the trespassing seems worse. Also, remember that grasshoppers lay eggs in late summer in the top 3 inches of the soil, so fall rototilling is good for destroying potentially threatening egg clusters.

A Grasshopper's Hope

Dear God, please hear the raspy song
I send out from my hiding place.
    My heart is lonely, and I long
    To see compassion on your face
Toward noisy bugs whose faith is strong,
Who hop through life from grace to grace.

My horns are long, so I look fierce,
But my green heart is full of fears.
    So come, warm God, hop to my side
    Until my terror disappears.
My feet are listening for your voice —
For that is where you put my ears.

I have no gift to speak or sing,
So I must pray with this rough tune:
    I scratch my leg across my wing
    And make love music to the moon,
And pray that leaps of faith will bring
Me to your presence, late or soon.

You taught me how to hop so high,
Now teach me how to hope in thee.
    You taught my heart to yearn to fly,
    Now give me deep humility.
You've bound me tight to earth and sky,
Now give me faith to set me free.

Dogs ~ BACKYARD THEOLOGY

The great theologian and author C.S. Lewis says that our animal companions may well be a part of our heavenly reward if we have formed a genuine relationship with them of caring and mutuality. His logic is simply that our ties to animals are unique relationships that possibly cannot be supplied in any other way. Fanciful as this thought may be, we may safely expect to be surprised by many things about the Next Life.

Hints for Lively Gardeners

Among the plants dangerous to dogs are poinsettias, mistletoe and philodendron. Also certain bulbs can make dogs ill: tulips, daffodils and iris, for instance. On the other hand, your garden plants are vulnerable to injury from dogs, so keep them away by fortifying the area with thorny hedges and forbidding plants. Roses, barberry, pyracantha, holly or gooseberry are bothersome enough to discourage the most determined canine intruders.

The Doggie's Dirge

A dog's life is forlorn, dear God,
Though we may leap and sport:
Our sorrow — and it breaks our hearts—
Is that our lives are short.

"A dog's best friend is man," they say,
"Or woman — saint or knave."
So dogs long to escort those lives
From childhood to the grave.

We live too fast! At three months old
We match a child of four.
At one, we're grown-up as our friend
Who is sixteen or more.
> In just two years we're as mature
> As humans twenty-five.
> And when we're ten, we're getting old
> And lucky to survive.

Please hear our prayer, forgive our need
To leap and bark and snort,
For we must cram a world of love
Into a life so short!

Dogma ~ Backyard Theology

The history of Christianity teaches us a lot besides dogma. Among other things, from the Christian past we learn to identify what in religion is essential and genuinely indestructible, what is most full of potential for either good or ill; and among other important things, we learn how to laugh at ourselves. People who constantly fret about dogma, for instance, and take great care to always be "orthodox" essentially imagine they can live in a textbook. Dogma (or official teaching) was never Jesus' preoccupation. He spoke of love, forgiveness, prayer and, above all, injustice. Of the dogmatists he quipped, "You strain out the gnat and swallow a camel."

 ## Hints for Lively Gardeners

Many garden and house plants are, unfortunately, harmful to cats. If your cat companion is an inveterate leaf chewer, to keep her/ him healthy it would be good to avoid plants like azaleas, chrysanthemums, oleander, philodendrons, daffodils, rhubarb and wisteria. Tell puss to concentrate on things marked "cat food" or items that appear in the designated dish.

A Cat's Dogma

The one thing I stay faithful to,
    The fruit of long research,
Is Dogma! Thank God it is sure:
    The Teaching of "the Church."

Some Liberals, flighty, hair-brained pets,
    Give in to every doubt.
They're called so *open-minded*
    That their brains are falling out.

Not me! I hold the Papal Bulls
    Infallible as God!
When bishops sit in council:
    Two great dogmas win my nod.

DON'T TRUST THE DOG! (Not thoroughbred,
    Nor mutt, nor cur, nor runt!)
WAIT FOR THE MOUSE! (He'll tiptoe out
    And save an irksome hunt.)

These are the dogmas I live by,
    My spiritual foundation.
Dogmatic cats live many lives,
    Nine's no exaggeration.

Pests ~ Backyard Theology

Like the pious aphid on the following page, are we expected to live with a willingness to die? Perhaps so. But that assumes also that we die for a reason, that there is meaning in death. Our aphid cousin knows that, in some circumstances, it is itself a pest and can only be such — at least from the gardener's perspective. So presumably it accepts its programmed demise as necessary. Can we not do the same? What kind of "good reason" or meaning could there be for our death? Even the Scriptural Job doesn't try to answer that question. He puts his hand over his mouth and surrenders. A model for aphids. And humans.

Hints for Lively Gardeners

Aphids are a great treat for ladybugs, who can eat up to 100 a day and still be hungry for more. You can order your ladybugs by mail, then keep them dormant in the refrigerator for 3 months or so and release only a few at a time. It isn't cruel at all. You can promise them the feast of a lifetime ahead. The aphids have learned over time to be pretty philosophical about it too. Could we not learn something from them?

The Pique of an Angry Aphid

"One of the least": that's me,
"Magnificent God": that's Thee!
　　How dare I flap my wings for your attention?
Still, I am moved to prayer
Partly because you're there
　　And I am here, almost too wee to mention.

Why do they call me "pest,"
When I just try my best
　　To play my role in this great cosmic dance?
Creation's wonderful!
No one's despicable!
　　All of us come from Love, and not from chance!

Some call me enemy,
and try to get rid of me,
　　Though I should rank sky high in their esteem:
First of all, I can fly!
Second, I *multiply*
　　Better than Einstein could in his wildest dream.
(Bisexual too, you know;
Twelve generations grow
　　In just one summertime, that's no extreme.)

Great God of Mystery,
Help human things to see
　　Reverence is due to all, both high and low,
Though they get rid of me,
To do it respectfully,
　　And only so more amazing life may grow.

Weeds ~ Backyard Theology

In the perspective of some people, heretics are the weeds growing in the Church, the ones Jesus called "tares." While fewer and fewer people these days are being openly called heretics (since from the Catholic perspective the official heretics, the Protestants, have settled down and built their own orthodoxies with heretics of their own), the inclination is still in us — in the human race — to condemn ideas that threaten us. In our own private hearts, do we not excommunicate many whose words sound threatening, the way weeds threaten a garden? How about the growing opposition of rich and poor: the poor are often blamed for their poverty, but so are the rich blamed for their wealth. Both may be innocent but perhaps simply uninformed. We need to cultivate that pure vision that Jesus spoke of and judge not, lest we be judged.

Hints for Lively Gardeners

If possible, water your garden before weeding it. Weeds are easier to pull with all their roots if the soil is moist. Also, plants nearby are less likely to be disturbed or damaged. Explain to your weeds that the sprinkling is to be a farewell pleasure; that, alas, life is short. Soak them well. They deserve a gentle departure.

The Tick's Fret

I hesitate, Great God Up There,
I'm such a creep! But hear this prayer.
   I ask you: Are your records straight
   In judging ticks' eternal fate?

Remember, we're those parasites
That include chiggers, nits and mites.
   (Too many, aren't we, Holy Maker?
   Sometimes 3 million to an acre!)

Confuse us not with folks around,
Whose names resemble ours in sound:
   Like here *TICS* of some persuasion
   Or even mys*TICS* on occasion.

That coterie of near namesakes
Are rightly damned for their mistakes!
   We fret! Might we come to perdition
   For misperceived name recognition?

We know misguided here*TICS*
Don't love the truth, like Catholics.
   And mys*TICS* often end in schism
   When they neglect their catechism.

Then ticks get daubed with the same paint
For things we never were and ain't!
   (Can one be sentenced to damnation
   For pure guilt-by-association?)

So please, dear God, don't mix our name
With wild freethinkers without shame.
   You'll find us ticks believe and do
   Whatever Dogma says is true.

Trash ~ Backyard Theology

The most outcast people in Jesus' time, those with leprosy, the "unclean," the "trash," were the very ones he sought out and befriended. That is a valid test of his authenticity — if one is familiar with the Hebrew Scriptures and its constant teaching that God cares most for those people most in pain. Isaiah told his listeners that the marginalized were their closest kin. That could only be true if God — speaking through prophets like Isaiah — conceives the human race as one family. Family members one would help first would be those in the greatest need. Today we have our own "unclean": the homeless poor in every city. Should we not do all we can for them?

Hints for Lively Gardeners

Stinkbugs — also known as harlequin bugs — love to suck the juice from the developing pods of okra and similar plants. The only known remedy is to pick them off by hand. But beware of giving them time to panic lest they start chemical warfare — which they are better at than you.

A Stinkbug's Wail

Unclean! Unclean! Great tenderhearted God,
Do not come near, we are an outcast race,
    The lepers of the insect world, the worst,
    Afflicted, feared and covered with disgrace!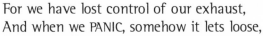

For we have lost control of our exhaust,
And when we PANIC, somehow it lets loose,
    A noxious, putrid, foul and horrid stink,
    A loathsome, vile and straight-from-hell-ish juice.

    Have mercy on yourself, Exalted Sovereign,
    And stay away from this, our last resort,
      Although we wish to link with other creatures,
      Yet only with each other dare consort.

What's that? What's that? You *like* our pungent odor?
You cooked it up on your computer screen?
    Diversity was what you hankered after?
    To teach that nothing created is unclean?

You've made us clowns, then, Harlequin of Heaven?
To make folks grin instead of cry in grief?
    Then give us grace to take ourselves more lightly,
    Contented to provide comic relief.

    Eternal Clown! Great Ocean of Surprises!
    Your sense of humor strengthens us to cope.
      While all our smiles be edged around with sadness,
      Still all our griefs have wistful tints of hope.

All right, come here where stinkbugs bow in worship,
Where red and blue and green clown-creatures crawl.
    Your Presence will improve our low self-image —
    Be careful! Don't cause PANIC in us all!

Depression ~ Backyard Theology

Is conflict and sorrow inevitable in life? Is there any other way to conceive of this earth but as a place of warfare, of animals eating living plants and chasing each other around — often with deadly intentions? As much as we wish for a milieu of total nonviolence, we don't live in one. Fleas do pester all our furry friends, and aphids do attack flowers and must be separated from them — as much as we may wish otherwise. Isn't this depressing? If it is, head for the garden, where you can have at least a symbolic, if partial, triumph over the forces of evil in the world.

Hints for Lively Gardeners

The best prayers have often been more groans than words, said John Bunyan (who made himself famous in saying it). Why? God reads the prayers in our hearts before we can utter them — and even if we do not utter them. If we go to the garden heavyhearted, we often return with a lighter step — with all our prayers said, or groaned.

Murmur of a Mournful Flea

Dear God, forgive the human race
For treating fleas like a disgrace,
Forgetting all the verve and flair
That make us fleas superb and rare.

We're *pulex irritans*, they bitch,
Which means "a louse that makes you itch."
Such talk is insulting as can be.
No! Wondrous miracles are we!

Yes, we are small, with tiny feet,
And little mouths you'd call petite,
And often bite off (sad but true)
A bit more than a flea can chew,
　　　Too small to breathe much oxygen:
　　　But not too small to say Amen!
(Our voice is somewhat hard to hear,
So we just whisper in God's ear.)

God, you don't find us bothersome,
Annoying, irritating, dumb,
Those ugly, irksome, pesky pests
That *pulex irritans* suggests.
　　　We're godlike insects born to jump,
　　　With sturdy hind legs, tough and plump,
With feathered forewings, made for prayer
Or streaking through the midnight air.

So bless us, Holy Mystery,
With more respect and courtesy
From mean, nitpicking humankind.
How boringly are *they* designed!
　　　All one! While God has made us fleas
　　　A thousand-plus varieties.
So we give praise, Love Unsurpassed,
Great Hairy God, our Home at last!

Bats ~ Backyard Theology

There are almost 900 kinds of bats! Mother Nature must be very convinced of the need for their presence. What about the 100,000 kinds of flies — and then many millions of each kind. What should we make of that? The Native Americans considered each phenomenon like this a Word of God. In a famous prayer, they would say, "Let my hands reverence all you have made and my ears be quick to hear your voice. Give me wisdom to understand all you have taught my people, to learn the lessons hidden in every leaf and rock. . ." and presumably in every bat and fly. Bats are particularly beneficial to humans and especially gardeners. They are a gardener's support staff. Why not welcome them and hear the Word of God they whisper?

Hints for Lively Gardeners

Be grateful for pest-devouring allies: bats, birds, frogs, lizards and spiders. Accommodate them in whatever way you can. For instance, draw spiders by planting asters and goldenrod, which spiders love for web sites (not the computer kind). In their webs they will trap many bugs and flies who may otherwise damage your crops.

The Curse of a Blasphemous Bat

I curse ye gods that walk the earth —
Called "womenfolk" and "men" —
   Who hate us bats before we have a chance
To demonstrate how beautiful and splendid bats can be,
   But put down our whole nation in advance.

I don't critique your godlike "kids," they usually respect us
   And love Bat-man, Bat-woman and Bat-child.
But as a rule you elders all abhor us and reject us,
   Not caring how we feel to be reviled.
We're mammals, folks! We nurse our babies just as humans do,
   So with *your* body-type we all comply.
You hate *our* looks? But what of yours? You lumber up and down,
   Pale, sluggish monsters who can't even fly!

Nine hundred kinds of bats are we, with technicolor coats
   Of black or red or yellow, gray or brown.
All night we ramble, guided by the echoes of our songs,
   At dawn sleep soundly, hanging upside down.

We're sunset lovers, quick as thought,
With sheer skin-covered wings,
   Our strong webbed fingers sculpturing our flight,
Our best have five-foot wingspans, live for twenty-five long years,
   Huge darts of darkness whizzing through the night!

So, all ye gods in human form, I've lost respect for thee,
And to your pride I dedicate this heartfelt blasphemy.

Birds ~ Backyard Theology

Why does this swallow think of God as the Supreme Bird, an eagle? For the same reason that male supremacist cultures (like ours) usually consider God to be male, and in fact, a wealthy land-owning male, a "lord." Only a male and a dominant person would be worthy to be God; a female God would be unworthy — since females are inherently inferior. On the other hand, every modern discipline that measures intelligence, good judgment and strength has established that the human sexes on earth are roughly equal. That calls for a change in the sky too. But don't tell the swallow — or the Church.

Hints for Lively Gardeners

Invite your favorite birds to your garden by building the houses of their dreams. Remember, martins and swallows prefer apartment-style houses, while wrens are reputed to favor sweet-smelling cedar homes. Bluebirds are drawn to lower houses — 5 feet off the ground — amid berry hedges. If possible, place all these houses at least 200 feet apart, however, to keep the peace, for many of these sweet-singing birds are fiercely territorial.

A Swallow's Tale

Long ago, Creator Eagle,
We would dress in ragged clothes,
Just some wandering bird freeloaders
On the backs of buffaloes.

Life was dusty, hot and boring,
Ticks and fleas our livelihood,
Till the show biz bug attacked us,
Drawing us to *Hollywood*!

Dressed, did we, in tails and linen,
Learned to soar and glide in style,
Somersaulting through the evening,
"*Swallow*ing" insects all the while.

Thus we joined your flying circus,
Doing tricks across the sky,
Astonishing the throngs below us,
Catching dinner on the fly.

Holy Eagle, calm and caring,
Bless your acrobats of space,
Joining your extravaganza:
Look! A miracle of grace.

Worms ~ Backyard Theology

Does God see us as we see ourselves? Hardly. We know ourselves as we are at this moment in time, but God sees what is eternally true: ourselves with all our potential and all our destiny. We may be seeing ourselves as inchworms, but God knows the butterfly we were born to become. And what is our name? God would probably not call us by the name we have on earth since it does not begin to name us in all we shall be. The fact is that the love of God surrounds and inhabits us, the wisdom of God inspires us and points us toward immense accomplishments. That's something that inchworms should to be thankful for — in advance.

Hints for Lively Gardeners

The adult moths we see near the lights on summer evenings are not necessarily our enemies. Many feed primarily on nectar and do little damage. Moth larvae — caterpillars — that feed on leaves do serious damage and should be picked off, gently, by hand. But wear gloves: Some have stinging hairs (just to remind you that your garden may be a lot more lively than you think).

The Hunch of an Inchworm

We hunch ahead, dear God, one inch a minute,
Slow but sure, we calmly do our thing.
Measuring our steps, so we will know the number
Of thanks we owe for your empowering.

We may not move as fast as others do,
But we get joy from dancing in a loop,
   Omega-shaped, then stretched out toward the future,
   Then with feet hunched again, forward we swoop.

Happy, we thrive, yet as we thrive we change!
Alas, we'll soon turn into moths who fly
   Uncalculated distances aloft,
   Infinite inches, up into the sky.

On that bright day, O God, may we remember
Each journey always with one small step starts,
   And trust that, though you once gave us but inches,
   You've dreams for us far greater than our hearts.

$\mathcal{S}$ex ~ Backyard Theology

Sex and sexuality is at the center of modern culture, but we have not yet paid enough attention to it. We can neglect its political implications. What political movement promoting change has more promise than has the movement for women's equality? Women hold fully 50% (and more) of the earth's pool of talent, intelligence, discernment and personal power — and it is not being used. No wonder our common world problems seem absolutely insoluble. We have tried every solution except through outright gender equality, putting all our powers to work.

Hints for Lively Gardeners

Sweet basil and sassafras are said to keep mosquitoes away. It is wise to plant them near doors, in window boxes or around patio edges. Also plant eucalyptus trees. Eucalyptus, besides repelling mosquitoes with their scent, require a lot of water and can help dry up boggy areas where mosquitoes breed. But remember, you have never had a mosquito "bite." You've just involuntarily donated blood to Little Ones. The Sisterhood is very grateful.

Mother Mosquito's Motet

Sing with bizz and buzz and zing
To the God of Everything,
Who has made mosquitoes proud
To rank high above the crowd.
    It's a female happening,
    When mosquitoes start to sing —
    Since the thirsting in our hearts
    Doesn't move male counterparts.

Valiant Sisters, then, are we
Giving thanks, O God, to thee,
Who has made us Mercy Nuns,
Drawing blood — for little ones,
    Not ourselves! We simply quest
    For blood donors — who are blest
    With a chance to do some good
    For the humble — as they should.

Alas, we've heard our caring rites
Falsely called "mosquito *bites*,"
No! Our hypodermic nose
Simply probes, then IN it goes!
    Out comes blood! We flash away
    Before a slap can spoil our day,
    And swim triumphant through the air,
    Home in time for evening prayer.

O Spirit, who makes all things new,
Give us strength and courage too
To ask the rich to share their grace,
To make this earth a better place.

Love ~ Backyard Theology

When one bug loves another — as lovebugs do all day and night — is that love? It seems to be. But it also seems not to be — or at least it should possibly have some other name. Still it looks just like a lot of human feelings called love. "The sight of you is thrilling. I love looking at you. Your shape, your scent attracts me. Your voice sounds like music. I want to be with you, close to you, linked to you!" What part of that is true love? Now add the human dimension: "I want you to be happy, to have enjoyment, to have pleasure, not to be in pain. I care what you say, what you think, how you sing, how you dance." Whatever this feeling may be called, it is an astonishing phenomenon. . . and it covers the earth from end to end.

Hints for Lively Gardeners

If you need to cover an area quickly and without spending a lot of money, purchase perennials that reseed easily. Good self-sowers include yarrow, lamb's ears, columbine, bellflower and pulmonaria. Imagine you are making one small space a model for the whole world, a sweet, healthy earth surrounded by fresh and bountiful air, washed by clean oceans and rivers, an earth covered with fragrant, colorful, friendly growing things that give each of us a sense that our homeland planet loves us and is honored to be our habitat for the few years of life we have.

The Love Bugs' Duet

Great Mystery of all mysteries above,
    Our thanks receive that we are bugs with *love*.
Among the feats we're widely famous for:
    Five days our life, we mate for two or more!

As soon as we can crawl we find a mate,
    Forgetting food, rest, travel: All can wait
While love exerts its strong resistless charm,
    O God, we thank thee: Keep us safe from harm!

Our choice: to love — or die? We choose the first
    And nothing else gets done — although we thirst
For knowledge, insight, virtue, discipline:
    We leave to you our lives that might have been.

We're made for love, an image near divine,
    A pair of bugs duetting and supine,
Singing our prayers of praise to you above
    While making out below, fast linked in love.

Growth ~ Backyard Theology

Are we willing to change, to improve? Cardinal Newman remarked that to improve means to have changed often. To give up on becoming more fully yourself, on contributing more meaningfully to the human enterprise, is a luxury we cannot indulge in, for it is essentially suicidal. We are hardly at that point. We may ask God for the gift of change, if that is something we really want. The pre-Christian Roman philosopher Seneca wrote: "We often want one thing and pray for another, not telling the truth even to the gods." Tell the truth to God. Decide today you are going to grow — a little each day, the way everything grows.

Hints for Lively Gardeners

Earthworms love coffee grounds. Bury grounds in a vegetable garden or a rose bed. Grounds provide nutrients and also discourage problematic visitors like slugs and grubs. In apple orchards, apples that are dimpled and tunneled with brown trails show signs that apple maggots, or "railroad worms," have been working. Some growers trap the egg-laying female maggots by hanging red croquet balls coated with commercial insect adhesive in their trees. Whatever your choices, ultimately you want to promote the Larger Life. That's what this world, this garden, is about.

The Maggot's Magnificat

With all my noble maggot's soul
    I magnify you, God,
And call your works all wonderful,
    Though scoffers find that odd.

"You legless grub, you loathsome worm,"
    They shout: "You're so inferior!"
"You have no head, yet eat all day,
    And breathe through your posterior!"

Dear God, how blind! — to criticize
    The magic of creation,
Where maggots raise flesh from the dead
    Through transubstantiation.

How beautifully the cycle spins
    When beings eat each other,
And one loved creature seems to die,
    Then rises in another.

Not only rises, but grows wings
    And soon begins to soar
Throughout the azure sky above
    And sings at heaven's door.

So with this grateful grubby heart
    I honor my Creator,
Who gives us death so we can then
    Turn into something greater.

Justice ~ Backyard Theology

Mystery God of Justice and Compassion, guide my heart in helping to build on this earth the ever-new Jerusalem. You are closest to us and most intimately involved in our lives when we work for fairness, justice and equality, when we campaign for just wages, just working conditions, just health care for all, a just care for our earthly home and just treatment of all, especially the most easily overlooked. Caring Mother of the Human Family, who fills the world with a plentitude of food, Caring Father, who watches over each child in pain or in danger, Mysterious God, in whom we live and move and have our being: guide us to labor in this world's Garden where our hands and skills are most needed — so we may have a part in the survival of the Earth and in the harvest of justice to come. Amen.

Hints for Lively Gardeners

A useful instrument of justice in your garden can be a scissors. Weeds are encroachers. Scissors may be used for quick weeding and to thin shallow-rooted seedlings such as onions. Just snip away what's unwanted. Other thinning methods may pull up too many plants. Scissors also come in handy for cutting lettuce and spinach without fuss. Use the time saved for important minutes in your hammock.

A Termite's Turmoil

Hear my prayer, Great Nature's God,
Mysterious, elusive, odd.
This termite's lost in pondering:
Lead, Kindly Light: I'm following.

> I'm one of several thousand kinds
> Of termite creeps with one-track minds,
> Chewing through the woods' debris —
> Behold: my boring destiny.

The protozoa in my gut
Help me digest birch, ash, beechnut.
Whatever comes before my path
I transform into aftermath:
> Great trees that fall down now and then
> We process into earth again.
Whole houses, barns, fence posts and sheds,
We just recycle into shreds.

Alas, sometimes we undermine
Some lovely house of oak or pine,
With busy jaws that chew all night
Without a break, till morning's light.
> (It's not a life I'd wish on thee
> If I were God and thou wert me.)

Another trick: We can grow wings
When a lover calls or siren sings.
Then after sex our winglets wilt.
Then back to work — to work off guilt.

So, God, grant me some better dreams
With plans to *build* within my schemes,
So our mad chewing marathon
Might build up an earth worth living on.

A Gardener's Winter Prayer

Great Spirit, who has chosen me
To live to see my garden grow,
To know the joy of harvesting,
Then watch the rows fill up with snow.

My garden's frozen, brown and black,
My corn is gathered into sheds,
I've harvested the winter squash,
I've tucked the crocus in their beds.

The rim within this old straw hat
Is damp with sweat from summer chores.
The price we pay to make things grow
Since we were barred from Eden's doors.

Life-Giving Spirit, now I'll rest
Just as my lively garden does,
Knowing if I've another spring
Life will return the way it was.

But should I feel the hand of death
Waking me to another sky,
Just like my garden, I will trust
There'll be a Springtime by and by.

*For as the earth puts forth her sprouts and as a garden makes the seed to spring up, **so shall God make justice and praise to spring up** before all nations. –* Isaiah 61: 11

*You crown the year with your **bountiful harvest,** and your carts overflow with abundance. The grasslands of the desert overflow. The hills are clothed with gladness. –* Ps. 65: 12

Author's Postscript:
The Destiny of Manure

Among the deeper mysteries of life is the mystery of manure: how awful it smells, how disgusting it looks, how repulsive it feels — yet how delicious it is to our vegetable cousins in the garden: the tomatoes, the corn, the carrots.

We put manure right into their bed. They not only welcome it, but they take it in, and through the life powers within them, absorb its very substance into their individual beings, transforming its smelly and disgusting substance miraculously into bright shining red tomatoes, yellow luscious corn, sweet wholesome carrots.

Miraculously, that execrable manure has now turned into something humans can eat: nourishing, sweet-smelling food, delicious to the mouth and life-giving to every part of our bodies — a magic we might expect to find only in mythical Eden.

Even more: Once we digest the food that nourished itself on manure, the atoms that once constituted manure quickly turn into us, turn into cells that taste and see and hear, muscle cells that can sculpt and play Chopin, nerve cells that can learn languages, remember things for more than eighty years and create imaginary worlds filled with marvelous fictional beings. Out of manure comes the human race and all our race does and can do.

What is more, the destiny of every human body, once it has exhausted its powerful life forces, is to *become* manure.

Passing strange but true. Mother Nature, in addition to welcoming the waste that we animal beings cast off daily, wants, at the end of life, to invite the deceased human body to become a part of the earth itself and a rich source of substances that can be transformed into plants and eventually into new animals and humans again. That's the only way life can go on.

Do we need to invent a system of human burial that is more ecologically enlightened? Ideally, we should bury our dead beneath a garden of thrilling flowers or thriving vegetables, or among the roots of fruitful trees. Thus within a few years, the beloved deceased bodies can reappear as living beings once again, and be resurrected into items as useful as apples and pears, corn and potatoes, crocus or chrysanthemums.

"Remember, thou art dust, and unto dust thou shalt return," say Christian priests on Ash Wednesday as they mark each human forehead with ashes. More accurately they should say, "Thou art manure, and unto manure thou shalt return." That would be a reminder of an honorable destiny indeed.

Plants, we know, love to live close to people partly because they breathe in our exhalations as we do theirs. The same is true of Mother Earth: She loves us because we are an essential part of her, and her fruits and vegetables are destined to be an essential part of us.

We are the earth, in fact — as much as any earthen lode of iron or copper, or molten mass of magma, or rainforest or desert. We are earth's very self, expressed particularly in human intelligence, energy, desire and bodiliness — as geologian Thomas Berry reminds us. So we have no nobler mission on earth than to be its caretakers and gardeners, midwifing the earth's energies for the benefit of all life. May it be so forever.